# tiny tastes &
# Mini Bites

Recipes by Thierry Roussillon
Photographs by Akiko Ida

HACHETTE
Illustrated

# contents

# come round for drinks...

## The scene's a familiar one.

A few weeks ago, you were invited round to friends for nibbles and drinks, so naturally you've invited them round to yours this time. The problem is that your friends are great cooks and even something as simple as cocktails has become a gourmet affair in their hands, so inviting them round can be daunting. Of course your friendship doesn't just depend on culinary skills, but if you're having them round, it should be special because they are special. After all, nothing is more unwelcoming than drinks served with bowls of uninspiring peanuts, dull old potato chips, or some other doubtful snack whose exact ingredients cannot be completely identified.

## Your options:

❯ Buy ready-made party food – but everyone will know where it came from.

❯ Back out and cancel the invitation.

❯ Get cooking – all you need are a few ideas and a little time.

**WARNING**
This book contains dishes that are made with raw or lightly cooked eggs. These should be avoided by vulnerable people such as pregnant and nursing mothers, invalids, the elderly, babies and young children.

## ❯ Hold the peanuts...

1 Turn the invitation to drinks into a light supper invitation. The atmosphere is always more relaxed than a dinner party and it's much simpler to prepare and easier on the waistline.

2 Choose a selection of 4–5 items that can be prepared shortly before your guests arrive. Make sure the only job you have to do once they've arrived is a bit of reheating.

3 Culinary boundaries have been pushed back and, no matter how unusual, most of the ingredients called for in this book are available in large supermarkets. Take the time to investigate the shelves thoroughly the next time you go shopping, and check out the gourmet sections which have a wealth of interesting items that are ideal for entertaining.

4 Have a well-stocked herbs and spice shelf to raid, including oregano, curry powder, basil, poppy seeds, sesame seeds, paprika etc.

5 The tastiest canapés are often the most simple, and these rely on top-quality ingredients. Bread is the starting point for most, so be sure to buy the best and experiment with different varieties: walnut bread, olive bread, rustic country loaves, ciabatta, pitas, dried fruit breads, seeded rolls and baps – the choice available is quite awesome.

6 Some of the recipes take only a few minutes to prepare, others take a little bit longer, but one thing is for certain – they can all be prepared in advance.

7 If it's a family gathering, remember to include some simple snacks, perhaps made in amusing shapes, to keep the youngest members happy.

# >a few suggestions for themed menus

## Italian
salami, cherry tomato, and Parmesan canapés (page 6)
Parma ham and black olive tapenade canapés (page 7)
beef carpaccio and oregano canapés (page 8)
Italian style phyllo pastries (page 14)
potatoes with beef carpaccio (page 28)

## Spanish
chorizo canapés (page 6)
empanadas with beef (page 18)
empanadas with cheese (page 18)

## Tex-Mex
guacamole and crunchy carrot canapés (page 30)
Mexican dips for tortilla chips (page 34)

## Provençal
pesto and anchovy canapés (page 10)
garlic mayonnaise canapés (page 10)
Niçoise mini sandwiches (page 42)
anchovy cream savory pastries (page 49)

## Mediterranean
Eggplant and feta phyllo pastries (page 15)
lamb and ginger mini kabobs (page 52)
falafel (page 58)

## Spicy kabobs
coconut-honey pork kabobs (page 52)
chicken satay (page 55)
mango-chile duck kabobs (page 56)

## Rustic
empanadas with Roquefort and hazelnuts (page 20)
potatoes with cured ham and cheese (page 28)
gourmet sandwiches (page 44)
blue cheese and pear mini tarts (page 46)

## Seafood
tuna carpaccio and basil canapés (page 8)
minted mussel stuffed shells (page 26)
scallops with basil stuffed shells (page 26)
apple and scallops with curry mini tarts (page 46)
scallops and bacon mini kabobs (page 54)
spicy shrimp kabobs (page 54)

## Vegetarian
stuffed cherry tomatoes (page 32)
chicory and blue cheese canapés (page 33)
curry-mustard sauce for cucumbers (page 36)
tartare sauce for cauliflower (page 36)
soft goats' cheese and tomato mini tarts (page 47)

## Children
Ham mini pizzas (page 12)
empanadas (page 18)
mini sandwiches( page 42)
fresh pea tortillas (page 50)
twisty pastry sticks (page 60)

## Chorizo

{
makes 8
preparation time: 10 minutes
cooking time: 5 minutes

1/2 baguette
1 garlic clove
olive oil
8 thin slices chorizo
8 thin slices hard cheese
black pepper

> IN ADVANCE

Slice the baguette into 8 canapé-
size rounds. Rub each with the garlic
clove and then drizzle with a little
olive oil.

Dry-fry the chorizo in a nonstick
skillet over low heat until just sizzling.
Top each bread round with a slice
of cheese, then a chorizo slice.

> JUST BEFORE SERVING

Preheat the oven to 400°F. Line a
cookie sheet with baking parchment.
Arrange the canapés on the sheet
and bake just until the cheese begins
to melt, about 1 minute. Sprinkle with
freshly-ground black pepper and
serve hot.

Note
Try a tasty sheep's milk cheese such
as Ossau-Iraty from the Pyrénées.
If this is not available, use Emmental,
Cantal or Cheddar.

## Salami, cherry tomatoes, and Parmesan

*great ✱✱✱*

{
makes 8
preparation time: 10 minutes
cooking time: 5 minutes

1/2 baguette
1 garlic clove
olive oil
4 cherry tomatoes, halved
8 small slices Italian salami
8 Parmesan shavings
salt and pepper

> IN ADVANCE

Preheat the broiler. Cut the baguette
into 8 canapé-size rounds. Toast
under the broiler, then rub each
slice with the peeled garlic clove and
drizzle with a little olive oil.

> TO SERVE

Halve the cherry tomatoes. Place a
salami slice on each round of toast,
then top with a Parmesan shaving
and half a cherry tomato. Season
and serve immediately.

> TO SERVE LATER

Cover the canapés with clingfilm
and refrigerate until needed.

Note
Use a vegetable peeler to slice neat
shavings from a block of Parmesan.

# Parma ham and black olive tapenade

makes 8
preparation time: 10 minutes
cooking time: 5 minutes

1/2 baguette
1 garlic clove
olive oil
2 slices Parma ham
1 small jar tapenade (black olive paste)
8 basil leaves
salt and pepper

> IF YOU'RE IN A HURRY

Prepare the bread as for the recipes on page 6.

> IF YOU HAVE MORE TIME

Cut the baguette into 8 canapé-size rounds. Rub the slices with garlic and then drizzle with a little olive oil. Toast the bread slices under a low broiler for 4–5 minutes, until they are really crisp.

> JUST BEFORE SERVING

Cut each ham slice into four. Spread tapenade on each round of toast, then top with a piece of ham and a basil leaf. Season.

> TO SERVE LATER

Cover with clingfilm and refrigerate until needed.

Note
Any other type of cured ham (prosciutto) can be used in place of the Parma ham.

# Beef carpaccio and oregano

{
makes 8
preparation time: 10 minutes
cooking time: 5 minutes

1/2 baguette
1 garlic clove
olive oil
8 small slices beef carpaccio
dried oregano
salt and pepper

> IN ADVANCE

Preheat the broiler. Slice the baguette into 8 canapé-size rounds. Toast under the broiler, then rub each slice with the peeled garlic clove and drizzle with a little olive oil.

> JUST BEFORE SERVING

Top each round of toast with a slice of carpaccio and sprinkle with oregano. Season with salt and pepper.

> TO SERVE LATER

Refrigerate until needed.

Note
You can replace the oregano with basil. Beef carpaccio is very thinly sliced beef, eaten raw. It must be very fresh and comes prepacked in delicatessens or from most supermarkets.

# Tuna carpaccio and basil

{
makes 8
marinating time: 1 hour
preparation time: 10 minutes
cooking time: 5 minutes

8 wafer-thin slices fresh tuna
olive oil
lemon juice
salt and pepper
1 sprig fresh basil leaves, finely shredded
1 teaspoon crushed peppercorns
1/2 baguette

> ONE HOUR IN ADVANCE

Arrange the tuna slices in a shallow dish. Drizzle with olive oil and lightly sprinkle with lemon juice. Season with salt and pepper, shredded basil and half the peppercorns. Marinate for 1 hour. If you can find pink peppercorns, they will make that extra difference.

> JUST BEFORE SERVING

Preheat the broiler. Cut the baguette into 8 canapé-size rounds and toast under the broiler. Remove the tuna from the marinade and arrange on top of the rounds of toast. Sprinkle with the remaining crushed peppercorns. Season to taste.

> TO SERVE LATER

Refrigerate until needed.

Note
Use smoked salmon in place of the tuna.

## Garlic mayonnaise

*Very Good*

makes 8
preparation time: 40 minutes
cooking time: 5 minutes

**Garlic mayonnaise**
6 garlic cloves
2 egg yolks
salt and pepper
1 3/4 cups olive oil
2 tablespoons lemon juice

1/2 baguette
8 slices cucumber
4 cherry tomatoes, halved

### IN ADVANCE

To make the garlic mayonnaise: peel the garlic cloves and crush in a garlic press or in a pestle and mortar. Transfer to a large bowl. Add the egg yolks and season with salt and pepper. Whisk in the oil, a drop at a time, until mixture thickens. Stir in lemon juice to taste. If the mayonnaise is too thick, thin with 1–2 teaspoonfuls warm water.

### JUST BEFORE SERVING

Preheat the broiler. Cut the baguette into 8 canapé-size rounds and toast under the broiler. Spread each slice with garlic mayonnaise, then top with slices of cucumber and the cherry tomatoes.

Note
Any leftover garlic mayonnaise can be served as a dip, accompanied by crunchy fresh vegetables (such as carrot, celery, cauliflower florets etc.).

## Pesto and anchovy

makes 8
preparation time: 10 minutes
cooking time: 5 minutes

1/2 baguette
1 garlic clove
1 small jar ready-made pesto
8 canned anchovy fillets, rinsed
pepper

### IN ADVANCE

Preheat the broiler. Cut the baguette into 8 canapé-size rounds. Place on a cookie sheet and toast under the broiler on one side only.
Rub the untoasted sides with garlic, then spread with a thin layer of pesto. Top each with an anchovy fillet and sprinkle with freshly-ground pepper.

### JUST BEFORE SERVING

Preheat the oven to 400°F. Line a cookie sheet with baking parchment. Place the canapés on the cookie sheet and bake for 5 minutes.
Serve warm, when the canapés have crisped up a bit.

Note
Try topping with chopped anchovies if a whole fillet seems too strong.

# Gorgonzola cream and walnuts

makes 8
preparation time: 10 minutes
cooking time: 5 minutes

1/4 cup crumbled Gorgonzola cheese
1 tablespoon mascarpone cheese
8 walnut halves
1/2 baguette
salt and pepper

> **PREPARATION**

In a shallow dish, blend the Gorgonzola and mascarpone cheeses with a fork. Crush half the walnuts and stir in. Check the seasoning.

> **JUST BEFORE SERVING**

Preheat the broiler. Cut the baguette into 8 canapé-size rounds and toast under the broiler. Spread each slice with the cheese mixture, then top with a piece of walnut.

> **TO SERVE LATER**

Refrigerate until needed.

Note
You can replace the mascarpone with thick sour cream, and the Gorgonzola with any other sort of blue cheese.

# With mussels

makes about 18
preparation time: 20 minutes
cooking time: 15 minutes

18–20 large mussels
1 packet ready-made pizza dough
1/2 garlic clove
1 jar pizza sauce
1 tablespoon olive oil
salt and pepper
dried oregano
a few shavings of Parmesan

### ❯ IN ADVANCE

Clean the mussels. Put in a pan with a little water, cover with a lid, and cook over low heat until the mussels begin to open. When cool enough to handle, remove the mussels from their shells. Discard any that haven't opened.

Unroll the pizza dough. Using a small round cookie cutter or a glass, cut 18 circles from the dough. Line a cookie sheet with baking parchment and arrange the dough circles on the sheet.

Crush the garlic clove and stir into the pizza sauce, along with the olive oil. Season well.

### ❯ ASSEMBLING THE PIZZAS

Spread a layer of pizza sauce on each dough circle and sprinkle with oregano. Top each pizza with a mussel and a Parmesan shaving.

### ❯ JUST BEFORE SERVING

Preheat the oven to 400°F.
Bake for 10–15 minutes. If not serving immediately, bake for a shorter time to allow for reheating without drying out. Serve hot.

Note
Use mussels in jars, or frozen mussels, to save time. Mussels in jars should be rinsed and drained before use. (Follow manufacturer's instructions for defrosting.)

# Variations

### Mushroom mini pizzas

Clean 3–4 mushrooms, remove the stems, and slice thinly. Spread the dough circles with the tomato sauce, cover each with a few mushroom slices, and some mozzarella cheese. Sprinkle with finely shredded fresh basil and season.

### Ham mini pizzas

Instead of mussels and Parmesan, top with ham, preferably a cured Italian ham, such as Parma or San Daniele. Cover each sauce-coated dough circle with slices of ham and sprinkle with oregano, salt, and pepper. Bake for 7 minutes. Serve hot.

## Italian style

makes 8
preparation time: 20 minutes
cooking time: 10 minutes

4 tomatoes, peeled and seeded
4 oz mozzarella
4 sheets phyllo pastry
2 sprigs fresh basil leaves,
thinly shredded
olive oil, for frying
salt and pepper

> IN ADVANCE

Finely chop the tomatoes. Cut the mozzarella into cubes. Cut each sheet of **phyllo** in half with scissors. Using your fingers, moisten each half with cold water.

> JUST BEFORE SERVING

Spread each half **phyllo** sheet with some chopped tomato. Top with mozzarella cubes, shredded basil and seasoning. Fold the **phyllo**, wrapping to completely enclose the filling, sealing the edges.

> DON'T FORGET TO WEAR AN APRON...

Heat some olive oil in a pan until a cube of bread turns brown in 30 seconds. Add the **phyllo** parcels and cook until golden. Drain on paper towels. Serve hot.

Note
If you don't have time to prepare fresh tomatoes, use canned peeled tomatoes instead. Be sure to drain them well.

## Chicken and prune

makes 8
soaking time: 2 hours
preparation time: 10 minutes
cooking time: 35 minutes

6 prunes, pitted
1 mint tea bag
1 skinless, boneless, chicken breast
1 onion
2 sprigs fresh cilantro, chopped
1/2 cup slivered almonds
4 sheets phyllo pastry
olive oil
salt and pepper

> IN ADVANCE

Soak the prunes in a bowl of mint tea. Finely chop the chicken and onion. Place in a pan with a little olive oil and cook until just brown, 2–3 minutes. Add the prunes, a few drops of the tea, and the chopped cilantro. Season, then cover and cook gently for 20 minutes. In another pan, dry-fry the almonds.

> JUST BEFORE SERVING

Cut the **phyllo** sheets in half with scissors and, using your fingers, moisten with cold water. Spread each half **phyllo** sheet with the chicken mixture and a few almonds. Fold the filo, wrapping to completely enclose the filling, sealing the edges. Cook in hot olive oil as for previous recipe. Serve immediately, or reheat in the oven before serving.

Note
Try replacing the prunes with dried apricots.

# Eggplant and feta cheese

makes 8
preparation time: 15 minutes
cooking time: 50 minutes

eggplant caviar (see recipe page 16)
1 cup crumbled feta cheese
4 tablespoons lemon juice
1 garlic clove, crushed
ground cumin
4 sheets phyllo pastry
olive oil for frying
salt and pepper

> **IN ADVANCE**

In a bowl, combine the eggplant caviar, feta cheese, lemon juice, garlic and cumin to taste. Mix thoroughly with a fork.

> **JUST BEFORE SERVING**

Cut each **phyllo** sheet in half with scissors. Use your fingers to moisten each sheet with cold water, to keep them supple.

Spread each **phyllo** sheet with the aubergine mixture. Fold the filo, wrapping to completely enclose the filling, sealing the edges. Heat some olive oil in a pan until a cube of bread turns brown in 30 seconds. Fry the parcels in the hot oil until golden. Drain on paper towels. Serve hot.

> **IF YOUR GUESTS ARE LATE**

Reheat in a warm oven for a few minutes.

# Eggplant caviar

makes 18
preparation time: 25 minutes
cooking time: 30 minutes

1 eggplant
squeeze of fresh lemon juice
1 garlic clove, crushed
2 sprigs fresh cilantro, chopped
olive oil
18 mini pita breads
salt and pepper

### ❯ IF YOU HAVE THE TIME

Preheat the oven to 350°F.

Wash the eggplant, cut in half lengthwise and make several slits in the flesh with a knife. Drizzle with some olive oil and wrap in aluminum foil. Bake in the preheated oven for about 30 minutes. Remove from the oven and scoop out the flesh.

In a bowl, combine the eggplant flesh, lemon juice, garlic and chopped cilantro leaves. Mix well with a fork. Gradually blend in the oil, a little at a time, until the caviar is the right consistency. It should be spreadable, but not too oily. Season well.

### ❯ JUST BEFORE SERVING

Fill the mini pitas. with the eggplant caviar.

### ❯ TO SERVE LATER

Refrigerate until ready to serve.

Note
If you are pressed for time, use ready-made eggplant caviar.

# Variations

### Red bell pepper pitas

Preheat the oven to 350°F.

Arrange whole red bell peppers on a roasting rack set over a roasting pan. Bake until the skins begin to blacken, about 45 minutes. Remove from the oven and put in a plastic bag to sweat.

After 10 minutes, remove from the bag and peel off the skins. Allow to cool, slice open and remove the seeds and core.

Put the bell pepper flesh in a food processor or blender and mix until smooth, or rub through a strainer. Add some olive oil, garlic, and seasoning. Refrigerate until required.

### Tzatziki pitas

Peel 1 medium cucumber. Slice in half lengthwise, salt and let stand for 1 hour to drain. Rinse and pat dry, then grate the cucumber.

Peel a garlic clove and chop finely.

In a bowl, combine the cucumber, 2 small pots Greek-style yogurt, the garlic, chopped fresh mint, and 2 tablespoons olive oil. Check the seasoning. Refrigerate until required.

# With cheese

makes 10
preparation time: 15 minutes
cooking time: 15 minutes

1 packet ready-made savory plain pastry dough
10 slices Emmental or mild cheddar
1 egg yolk
pepper
poppy seeds

> IN ADVANCE

Preheat the oven to 400°F.

Unroll the pastry dough and cut out 10
circles, 2 1/2 inches in diameter, with a glass
or a cookie cutter. Break the cheese slices
into small pieces.

> JUST BEFORE SERVING

Put cheese pieces on one half of each circle.
Season with pepper. Dampen the edges
and fold over, sealing the edges firmly.

Whisk the egg yolk with a little water and
brush on one side of the pastry parcels..
Sprinkle a few poppy seeds on top of the
egg glaze.

Line a cookie sheet with baking parchment.
Arrange the empanadas on the sheet and
bake in the preheated oven for 10–15
minutes, until golden. Serve hot.

Note
You can also add dried fruit and nuts to the
filling (such as raisins, dried apricots,
walnuts, almonds etc.).

# With beef

makes 10
preparation time: 20 minutes
cooking time: 20 minutes

1 packet ready-made savory plain pastry dough
1 onion
4 large white mushrooms
3/4 cup ground beef
2 oz pine nuts
1 sprig thyme
1 egg yolk
sesame seeds
salt and pepper

> IN ADVANCE

Preheat the oven to 400°F.

Unroll the pastry dough and cut out 10
circles, 2 1/2 inches in diameter, with a glass
or a cookie cutter.

Chop the onion and the mushrooms finely.

In a bowl, combine the beef, onion,
mushrooms and pine nuts. Add the thyme
leaves, salt and pepper, and mix well. Put a
little oil to heat in a pan and fry the mixture
for a few minutes until the meat is cooked.

> JUST BEFORE SERVING

Put a little of the meat filling on one half of
each pastry circle. Dampen the edges and
fold over, sealing the edges firmly. Whisk the
egg yolk with a little water and brush on one
side of the pastry parcels. Sprinkle a few
sesame seeds on top of the egg glaze.

Line a cookie sheet with baking parchment.
Arrange the empanadas on the sheet and
bake in the preheated oven for 10–15
minutes, until golden. Serve hot.

## With Roquefort and hazelnuts

makes 12
preparation time: 20 minutes
cooking time: 20 minutes

1 packet ready-made savory plain
pastry dough
1 cup crumbled Roquefort cheese
24 hazelnuts, crushed
sour cream
1 egg yolk
salt and pepper

### ❯ IN ADVANCE

Preheat the oven to 400°F.

Unroll the pastry dough and cut out
10 circles, 2¹/₂ inches in diameter,
with a glass or cookie cutter.

Put the cheese and hazelnuts in a
bowl and mix together thoroughly
with a fork. Add a little sour cream
to thin, if necessary.

### ❯ JUST BEFORE SERVING

Put a little cheese filling on one half
of each pastry circle. Dampen the
edges and fold over, sealing the edges
firmly. Whisk the egg yolk with a little
water and brush on one side of the
pastry parcels. Line a cookie sheet
with baking parchment. Put the
empanadas on the sheet and bake in
the preheated oven for 10–15
minutes, until golden. Serve hot.

Note
Try using Bleu de Bresse cheese
instead of Roquefort, and replace
the hazelnuts with almonds.

## With ratatouille

makes 10
preparation time: 15 minutes
cooking time: 20 minutes

1 packet ready-made savory plain
pastry dough
8 oz ratatouille
2 tablespoons ready-made pesto
1 egg yolk
salt and pepper

### ❯ IN ADVANCE

Preheat the oven to 400°F.

Unroll the pastry dough and cut out
10 circles, 2¹/₂ inches in diameter
with a glass or cookie cutter.

In a bowl, combine the ratatouille
and pesto. Check the seasoning and
adjust if necessary.

### ❯ JUST BEFORE SERVING

Put a little ratatouille filling on one
half of each pastry circle. Dampen
the edges and fold over, sealing the
edges firmly. Whisk the egg yolk
with a little water and brush on
one side of the pastry parcels.

Line a cookie sheet with baking
parchment. Put the empanadas on
the sheet and bake for 15–20
minutes, until golden. Serve hot.

Note
This is a great way to use leftover
home-made ratatouille, but if you
don't have any, ready-made will do.

# With tuna

makes 10
preparation time: 20 minutes
cooking time: 20 minutes

1 packet ready-made savory plain
pastry dough
1 small can tuna in spring water
1 tomato, peeled, seeded,
and chopped
1 onion, finely chopped
1 egg yolk
salt and pepper

❯ IN ADVANCE

Preheat the oven to 400°F.

Unroll the pastry dough and cut out
10 circles 2 1/2 inches in diameter with
a glass or cookie cutter.

Drain the tuna well. Put the tuna in a
bowl together with the tomato and
onion. Season with salt and pepper
and mix well.

❯ JUST BEFORE SERVING

Put a little tuna filling on one half of
each pastry circle. Dampen the edges
and fold over, sealing the edges firmly.
Whisk the egg yolk with a little water
and brush on one side of the pastry
Line a cookie sheet with baking
parchment. Put the empanadas on
the sheet and bake for 15–20
minutes, until golden. Serve hot.

Note
To ring the changes, you can also
add canned sweetcorn, or finely
chopped red or green bell pepper
to the tuna.

## Chicken and tomato

makes 24 shells
preparation time: 20 minutes
cooking time: 30 minutes

olive oil
1/2 cup cooked chicken breast,
finely chopped
1 onion, peeled and finely chopped
1 garlic clove
1 tablespoon tomato paste
3 1/2 tablespoons dry white wine
1 level teaspoon chicken bouillon powder
24 large pasta shells
salt, coarse salt and pepper

### ❯ IN ADVANCE

Heat a little olive oil in a pan. Add the
chicken and cook until browned, then add
the onion and garlic. Stir well, then add
the tomato paste. Cover and cook for
10 minutes. Add the wine, bouillon powder,
and a 1/2 cup of water. Raise the heat and
cook for 20 minutes, or until the liquid is
almost completely evaporated.

### ❯ MEANWHILE...

Cook the pasta shells in a large pot of salted,
boiling water until al dente. Drain thoroughly.

### ❯ JUST BEFORE SERVING

Fill the shells with the chicken mixture and
serve immediately at room temperature.
Do not fill shells in advance.

Note
Very large pasta shells can be found in
Italian delicatessens and large supermarkets.
With any luck, you might even find some
colored varieties.

## Variations

### Salmon, sour cream and dill

Melt a little butter in a pan, add 1/2 cup
finely chopped fresh salmon. Cook for
5 minutes, stirring constantly, then add a little
sour cream and chopped fresh dill. Season
with salt and pepper and cook for more
5 minutes. Spoon into the pasta shells and
serve hot.

### Ham and mushrooms in bechamel sauce

Make some bechamel sauce (melt a knob
of butter in a small pan, add 1 teaspoon
all-purpose flour and cook for a minute or
two, then gradually add 1 cup milk and cook,
stirring, until the sauce thickens). Add 6 finely
chopped button mushrooms. Stir in 1 heaping
tablespoon grated Gruyère cheese, a pinch
of ground nutmeg ,and 1/4 cup finely chopped
ham. Season to taste and use to fill the
cooked pasta shells.

## with scallops

makes 20
preparation time: 15 minutes
cooking time: 20 minutes

1 1/4 cups dry white wine
4 small shallots, finely chopped
20 scallops
3/4 cup sour cream
curry powder
5 ready-made crêpes
salt and pepper

> IN ADVANCE

These can be assembled in advance, but reheat lightly before serving.

In a pan, combine the wine and shallots. Season and bring to a gentle boil.

Add the scallops and poach for 3 minutes. Remove and drain. Slice each scallop into three thin diskes. Stir the sour cream and some curry powder into the wine. Stir well, then cook over high heat until reduced by one-third. Remove from the heat.

> TO SERVE

Slice each crêpe into 4 strips.

Put 1 scallop diske on each crêpe slice, then spoon over some sauce. Fold the crêpe to enclose the filling. Hold in place with a toothpick. Serve hot.

Note
You can use frozen scallops if fresh are unavailable.

## Variations

### With mussels

Scrub 40 mussels. Put in a pan with 2 cups strong cider and steam until the shells open. Remove the mussels and reserve the cooking liquid. Discard any mussels that haven't opened. Strain the cooking liquid and put in a small pan. Stir in 2 tablespoons sour cream and 4 finely chopped shallots. Cook until reduced by half. Put 2 mussels on each crêpe slice and spoon over some sauce. Fold to enclose the filling. Hold in place with a toothpick. Serve hot.

Note
Use a coffee filter to strain the mussel cooking liquid.

### With apples and crab

Peel 2 apples and cut into small cubes. Cook in unsalted butter with 8 oz crab meat, stirring constantly, for 5 minutes.

Add 1/2 cup sour cream and a few drops of Tabasco. Allow to cook a few minutes more. Spoon a little of the crab mixture onto each crêpe slice and fold to enclose the filling. Hold in place with a toothpick.

Note
Other shellfish can be used in place of the crab.

## Minted mussels

makes 24
preparation time: 10 minutes
cooking time: 25 minutes

24 large mussels
2 tablespoons unsalted butter
2 tablespoons olive oil
1 garlic clove, crushed
2 cups fresh breadcrumbs
2 bunches fresh mint, chopped
salt, coarse salt and pepper

### ❯ IN ADVANCE

Wash and scrub the mussels
thoroughly. Put in a pan with a little
water, cover, and cook until the
shells open. Discard any shells that
don't open.

Spread a layer of coarse salt on a
cookie sheet. Arrange the cooked
mussels in the shells on top.

Melt the butter in a pan. Add the
olive oil, and garlic, and cook for
2 minutes. Stir in the breadcrumbs.
When the mixture has cooled, stir
in the mint and season.

### ❯ JUST BEFORE SERVING

Preheat the oven to 400°F.

Put a little of the breadcrumb
mixture on top of each mussel and
bake for 8–10 minutes. Serve hot

Note
You can replace the mint with herbes
de Provence.

## Scallops with basil

makes 24
preparation time: 5 minutes
cooking time: 15 minutes

24 scallops (with their shells)
olive oil
pine nuts
1 jar ready-made pesto
salt and pepper

### ❯ IN ADVANCE

Preheat the oven to 425°F.

Slice the scallops into thin diskes.

Heat a little olive oil in a skillet, add
the scallops, and cook until golden,
about 5 minutes. Dry-fry the pine
nuts in another skillet until golden.

### ❯ JUST BEFORE SERVING

Put 3 scallop slices into each scallop
shell. Top with a dollop of pesto and
season. Put in the hot oven for a few
minutes just to warm, sprinkle with
the pine nuts, and serve hot.

Note
Make sure the scallop shells have
been opened for you.

# Hot oysters with foie gras

makes 24
preparation time: 10 minutes,
plus the time it takes to open
the oysters
cooking time: 15 minutes

2 dozen oysters
12 thin slices pâté de foie gras
1 handful slivered almonds
salt, coarse salt and pepper

> **READY IN NO TIME, IF...**

You have already opened the oysters
and sliced the pâté de foie gras.

Preheat the oven to 425°F.

Spread a layer of coarse salt on a
cookie sheet. Arrange the oysters in
their shells on the salt and top each
with a slice of pâté de foie gras.
Season to taste.

Dry-fry the slivered almonds.

> **JUST BEFORE SERVING**

Bake in the hot oven for about
15 minutes. Sprinkle with slivered
almonds and serve immediately.

Note
Use cured ham or bacon in place of
the foie gras.

# With beef carpaccio

{
makes 20
preparation time: 10 minutes
cooking time: 20 minutes

10 small potatoes
20 slices beef carpaccio
1 teaspoon sesame seeds
1 bunch of fresh cilantro
salt, coarse salt, and pepper

❯ IN ADVANCE

Wash the potatoes, then steam without peeling for about 20 minutes, until tender. Trim the rounded ends, then cut into slices.

❯ JUST BEFORE SERVING

Top each potato slice with a slice of carpaccio. Sprinkle with sesame seeds and chopped cilantro.
This dish can easily be made in advance since it should be eaten cold.

Note
Use marinated fresh tuna in place of the carpaccio.

# Variations

{
## With smoked salmon

Cut 5 slices of smoked salmon into 4 thin slices each.
Top each potato round with a slice of salmon, a dollop of sour cream and salmon eggs. You can also decorate with fresh dill.

{
## With cured ham and cheese

Cut 2 oz cured ham into small cubes and 2 oz cheese, such as Reblochon or Brie, into thin slices.
Halve the steamed potatoes lengthwise, as for baked potatoes. Scoop out the flesh with a small spoon.
In a bowl, mix the potato flesh with the cubed ham and 1 teaspoon sour cream or yogurt. Season with salt and pepper.
Fill the potato shells with this mixture and top each with a slice of cheese. Brown under a preheated broiler until bubbling. Serve hot.

# Guacamole and crunchy carrots

> makes 20
> preparation time: 15 minutes
> cooking time: 10 minutes

2 avocados
1/2 onion, chopped
1/2 tomato, peeled, seeded, and chopped
2 teaspoons fresh lemon juice
1 teaspoon oil
Tabasco
2–3 large carrots
salt

### ❭ TO MAKE THE GUACAMOLE...

Halve the avocados, scoop out the flesh, and mash with a fork, or blend, until smooth.

In a bowl, combine the avocado, chopped onion, tomato, lemon juice, oi,l and a few drops Tabasco. Mix well, taste for seasoning, and adjust as necessary.

### ❭ THE CARROTS

Peel the carrots, cut into rounds and cook in boiling, salted water until just tender (the carrots should still retain some crunch). Set aside to cool, then top each round with a dollop of guacamole and serve.

Note
To save time, use ready-made guacamole, available in most supermarkets.

# Artichoke bottoms with fish mousse

> makes 20
> preparation time: 15 minutes
> cooking time: 15 minutes

1 lb cod fillet
2 cups crème fraîche (see note)
1 tablespoon lemon juice
20 small frozen artichoke bottoms, cooked, or from a jar
salt and pepper

### ❭ IN ADVANCE

Poach the cod fillet in a large pan of boiling, salted water for 15 minutes. Drain, then purée in a food processor. Season with salt and pepper.
Stir in the crème fraîche and lemon juice.

### ❭ JUST BEFORE SERVING

Fill the artichoke bottoms with the fish mixture. Refrigerate until ready to serve.

Note
For homemade crème fraîche, put 2 cups whipping cream and 4 tablespoons buttermilk in a glass container. Cover and let stand at room temperature (about 70°F) from 8 to 24 hours, or until very thick. Stir well before covering and refrigerate.

# Crunchy cucumber with crab

> makes 24
> preparation time: 10 minutes,
> plus 30 minutes draining

4 cucumbers
9 oz crab meat
2/3 cup mayonnaise
3 tablespoons lemon juice
1 bunch fresh mint, chopped
Tabasco
salt and pepper

> **PREPARE THE CUCUMBERS**

Wash the cucumbers. Peel, leaving
alternating stripes of dark green.
Cut into 1/2 inch thick slices. Sprinkle
with salt and leave on paper towels
to drain for 30 minutes.

> **MEANWHILE...**

In a bowl, combine the crab meat,
mayonnaise, lemon juice, chopped
mint, and a few drops Tabasco.
Mix well and check the seasoning.
Top each cucumber slice with a
spoonful of crab mixture.

Note
Decorate with whole mint leaves,
if you wish. Very small cucumbers
are also a good idea since they are
easier to eat with the fingers.

# Stuffed cherry tomatoes

> makes 24
> preparation time: 15 minutes

24 cherry tomatoes
1/2 cup crumbled feta cheese
1 tablespoon chopped fresh basil
1 teaspoon sour cream
pine nuts
salt and pepper

> **THE TOMATOES...**

Slice off the top of each tomato and
scoop out the flesh.

> **THE FILLING...**

In a shallow dish, combine the feta,
basil, sour cream, and mix well.
Season with salt and pepper.
Spoon the filling into each tomato,
sprinkle with pine nuts and replace
the tomato tops.

Note
You can use another type of soft
cheese, such as cream cheese, to
replace the feta.

# Belgian endive with blue cheese

makes 24
preparation time: 15 minutes

24 firm Belgian endive leaves
1/2 apple
1 scant cup crumbled blue cheese,
such as Roquefort or Stilton
3 1/2 tablespoons sour cream
a few slivered almonds

> IN ADVANCE

Peel the apple and cut into small
cubes.
In a shallow dish, mix together the
cheese and sour cream with a fork
until smooth. Stir in the apple cubes.

> JUST BEFORE SERVING

Spoon some of the mixture onto
the end of each leaf and sprinkle with
slivered almonds. Serve immediately.

Note
Try using a pear instead of the apple.

# Blue cheese dip

makes 1 bowl
preparation time: 15 minutes

1 cup crumbled Stilton cheese
3 1/2 tablespoons light cream cheese
3 1/2 tablespoons sour cream
1 onion, very finely chopped
salt and pepper

> IN ADVANCE

In a shallow dish, mash the Stilton with a fork,
then stir in the cream cheese, sour cream,
and chopped onion. Check the seasoning.
Transfer to a bowl and serve with cheese
flavored tortilla chips.

Note
Any type of blue cheese can be used in this
recipe.

# Cottage cheese dip

makes 1 bowl
preparation time: 10 minutes

1 scant cup cottage cheese
1 garlic clove, crushed
a few chives, finely snipped
pinch of cayenne pepper

> SIMPLY MIX

In a bowl, combine all the ingredients and mix
well. Serve with tortilla chips.

# Guacamole

makes 1 bowl
preparation time: 15 minutes

3 large avocados
1 onion, chopped
1 tomato, peeled, seeded, and chopped
4 teaspoons fresh lemon juice
2 teaspoons oil
Tabasco
salt

> USE RIPE AVOCADOS

Halve the avocados, scoop out the flesh, and
mash with a fork, or blend, until smooth.
In a bowl, combine the avocado, onion,
tomato, lemon juice, oil, and a few drops
Tabasco. Mix well and check the seasoning.
Serve in a bowl with tortilla chips.

Note
Ready-made guacamole is a time saver.

# Easy spicy dip

makes 1 bowl
preparation time: 10 minutes

Combine I scant cup cream cheese with
I teaspoon cayenne pepper, I tablespoon
Worcestershire sauce, salt, pepper, chopped
chives, and I teaspoon curry powder.
Mix well and serve in a bowl.

## Curry-mustard sauce for cucumbers

makes 1 bowl
preparation time: 15 minutes

4 cucumbers
1 scant 1/2 cup cream cheese
1 tablespoon curry powder
1 teaspoon Dijon mustard
salt and pepper

> IN ADVANCE

Peel the cucumber and cut into sticks.
Combine the remaining ingredients in a bowl.
Stir well and check seasoning. Serve chilled.

## Tomato mayonnaise for carrots

makes 1 bowl
preparation time: 20 minutes

1 egg yolk
1 teaspoon Dijon mustard
1 cup oil
2 teaspoon fresh lemon juice
1 tablespoon tomato paste
1 bunch of basil, chopped
carrots, cut into sticks
salt and pepper

> COULDN'T BE EASIER

Start with an egg yolk at room temperature
(the same as the oil). Put the egg yolk in a
bowl, add the mustard and stir well. Season,
then gradually whisk in the oil, by hand or
with a mixer, until completely blended and
thick. Stir in the lemon juice, tomato paste
and chopped basil. Serve with carrot sticks.

## Tartare sauce for cauliflower

makes 1 bowl
preparation time: 20 minutes
cooking time: 10 minutes

1 cauliflower, divided into florets
1 hard-cooked egg, yolk only
1 teaspoon Dijon mustard
1 cup oil
2 tablespoons lemon juice
1 bunch of chives, chopped
1 small onion, chopped
salt and pepper

> IN ADVANCE

Cook the cauliflower florets for 10 minutes
in boiling, salted water. Drain and set aside.

> MEANWHILE...

Mash the egg yolk with a fork. Stir in the
mustard. Season with salt and pepper, then
gradually whisk in the oil, by hand or with
a mixer, until completely blended and thick.
Stir in the lemon juice, chopped chives
and chopped onion. Check the seasoning.
Serve with the florets.

# Seaweed rolls

makes 20
preparation time: 30–45 minutes
cooking time: 15 minutes
equipment: bamboo rolling mat

nori seaweed sheets
1 2/3 cups vinaigered rice (see page 40)
wasabi
1 avocado, peeled and thinly sliced
4 crab sticks (surimi)
1/2 cucumber, cut into thin sticks
1 small jar salmon eggs
soy sauce, for serving

> ESSENTIAL EQUIPMENT

Lay a sheet of nori on the bamboo mat.
Spread over a layer of rice, then spread a
thin layer of wasabi on top. Arrange either
avocado slices, crab sticks, or cucumber
sticks, and salmon eggs on top.

> IT'S ALL IN THE WRIST

Roll up the nori to enclose the filling, using
the mat to push. Slice the roll into short
pieces. Repeat until all the filling ingredients
are used up.

Note
In place of vinaigered rice, use sticky rice
cooked in twice its volume of salted water.
Sticky rice is sold in Chinese supermarkets.
You can also use mayonnaise in place of
the wasabi.

# Variations

## With carrots

Place a sheet of nori on top of the bamboo
mat. Spread with a layer of vinaigered or
sticky rice.
Spread with mayonnaise, then top with a layer
of thin carrot sticks that have been blanched
in boiling salted water for a few minutes.
Roll up and cut into slices.

## With chicken

Poach a chicken breast in boiling, salted water
(or season with a stock cube). Slice thinly.
Place a sheet of nori on the bamboo mat,
spread with a layer of rice and top with a
thin coating of wasabi (or use mayonnaise
or whole-grain mustard). Arrange the chicken
slices on top.
Roll up and cut into slices with a sharp knife.

# Sushi

{
makes 20
preparation time: 30 minutes
cooking time: 15 minutes

3/4 cup Japanese mochi rice
1 cup water
2 tablespoons rice vinegar
1 teaspoon mirin (rice wine)
2 teaspoons sugar
2 teaspoons salt
2 slices smoked salmon, sliced into strips
1 small can tuna, drained
mayonnaise
chives, snipped with scissors
sesame seeds
wasabi
soy sauce

### ❯ THE RICE BIT

Rinse the rice thoroughly under cold running water. In a pan, combine the water, rice vinegar, mirin, sugar, salt, and rice. Bring to a boil, then reduce the heat and cook for 15 minutes. Allow to cool.

### ❯ GETTING IN SHAPE

Take small balls of rice and with your fingers shape them into rectangles. Cover half the rice rectangles with a slice of salmon. Mix the tuna with a little mayonnaise and spread on top of the remaining rice rectangles. Sprinkle each sushi with chives and sesame seeds. Serve with soy sauce and wasabi.

Note
In place of vinaigered rice, use sticky rice cooked in twice its volume of salted water. Sticky rice is sold in Chinese supermarkets.

# Variations

### With Parma ham

Prepare the rice as for the main recipe. Use your fingers to form the rice into rectangles, then top each with a slice of Parma ham and decorate with thin shreds of fresh basil.

### With lumpfish caviar

Prepare the rice as for the main recipe. Shape into rectangles, or another shape, with your fingers. Spoon some lumpfish caviar on top – use both red and black caviar and alternate the colors.

### Sweet sushi

Cook sticky rice in twice its volume of milk (sweetened with either vanilla sugar or honey). Allow to cool.
Shape the rice into rectangles and cover with slices of fresh fruit in season (strawberries, peaches, apples, pears, apricots, etc.) or use exotic fruit (mangoes, litchis, etc.).

# Niçoise

Makes 8
preparation time: 15 minutes

8 small crusty rolls
olive oil
24 cherry tomatoes
8 canned anchovy fillets, rinsed
1 onion, finely chopped
1/2 green bell pepper, thinly sliced
8 small black olives
salt and pepper

> **DON'T SLICE ALL THE WAY THROUGH**

Slice the rolls just to open and moisten with
olive oil. Quarter the cherry tomatoes and
slice the anchovies in half lengthwise.

Divide all the ingredients amongst the rolls
and fill. Season lightly with salt and pepper
and serve.

# Variations

## Mini burgers

In a shallow dish, combine 1/2 cup ground
beef and 1 chopped onion.

Shape into 8 thin, mini burgers. Cook in
a nonstick skillet.

Toast 8 small rolls, then slice open. Fill with
the mini burgers and garnish with ketchup,
thinly sliced pickles, lettuce leaves, and
cucumber and tomato slices.

## Mini hot dogs

Fry 1 chopped onion in some olive oil over
low heat until soft, about 10 minutes.

Cook 16 small frankfurters.

Toast some small rolls, spread with mustard
and fill with the fried onions and frankfurters.

## Assorted sandwiches

makes about 50–60
preparation time: 20 minutes
cooking time: 10 minutes

1 1/4 cups crumbled blue cheese
2 tablespoons sour cream
2 tablespoons chopped walnuts
5 oz fresh salmon
1 tablespoon salted butter
2 tablespoons lemon juice
2 oz smoked salmon, thinly sliced
1 loaf each brown and white bread, crusts
removed and thinly sliced
softened butter
4 thin slices prosciutto or Parma ham
salt and pepper

### BEFORE YOU START

Make the cheese and salmon fillings...

### CREAM OF BLUE CHEESE WITH WALNUT

In a shallow dish, use a fork to mash the
cheese, then stir in the sour cream and
walnuts. Set aside.

### TWO-SALMON PATÉ

Poach the fresh salmon in boiling salted water
for about 10 minutes. Drain and allow to
cool.
Flake the flesh and mix with the salted butter
and lemon juice. Stir in the smoked salmon
and check the seasoning.

### ACTION!

Prepare all the bread slices and divide into
3 groups. Fill the first with the blue cheese
mixture, the second with the salmon. For the
third, spread the bread with softened butter
and top with ham slices.

Note
A large round loaf, carefully hollowed out,
makes a novel container in which
to display the sandwiches.

## Variations

TRY THESE FILLINGS...
• BLT with mayo
• chorizo slices and cheese
• avocado and shrimp
• mozzarella and tomato

# Blue cheese and pear

{ makes 20
preparation time: 20 minutes
cooking time: 20 minutes

1 roll ready-made puff pastry dough
2 cups crumbled blue cheese
2 ripe pears

> BAKING BLIND

Preheat the oven to 440°F for 20 minutes. Roll out the dough and cut out 20 squares with a cookie cutter or a knife. Prick each square with a fork and place on a cookie sheet lined with baking parchment. Put another layer of baking parchment on top and weigh down with dried beans or pie weights. Bake for 15–20 minutes.

> MEANWHILE...

Crumble the cheese. Peel and cut the pears into very thin slices. Remove the pastry squares from the oven.

> JUST BEFORE SERVING

Sprinkle each pastry square with some blue cheese, then pop under a hot broiler just to melt. Top each with a slice of pear.

Note
Fourme d'Ambert cheese is especially delicious, but any other blue cheese works well.

# Apple and scallops with curry

{ makes 20
preparation time: 10 minutes
cooking time: 20 minutes

1 roll ready-made plain pastry dough
2 apples
24 scallops
unsalted butter
curry powder
salt

> BAKING BLIND

Preheat the oven to 440°F for 20 minutes. Roll out the dough and cut out 20 circles with a cookie cutter or small glass. Prick each circle with a fork and place on a cookie sheet lined with baking parchment. Put another layer of baking parchment on top and weigh down with dried beans or pie weights. Bake for 15–20 minutes.

> MEANWHILE...

Peel the apples and slice thinly. Cut each scallop into three thin circles, then place in a pan and cook gently in butter until golden. Season with salt.

> JUST BEFORE SERVING

Top each pastry with a slice of apple, a scallop circle, and sprinkle with curry powder. Reheat briefly just before serving.

Note
Use frozen scallops if fresh are unavailable.

# Soft goats' cheese and tomato

{
makes 20
preparation time: 20 minutes
cooking time: 25 minutes

1 roll ready-made plain pastry dough
1 cup) soft goats' cheese
7 tablespoons light cream
10 cherry tomatoes, halved
1 bunch of fresh mint, snipped
with scissors
salt and pepper

> **BAKING BLIND**

Preheat the oven to 440°F for 20 minutes. Roll out the dough and cut out 20 squares with a cookie cutter or a knife. Prick each square with a fork and place on a cookie sheet lined with baking parchment. Put another layer of baking parchment on top and weigh down with dried beans or pie weights. Bake for 15–20 minutes.

> **MEANWHILE...**

In a shallow dish, combine the goats' cheese and cream and season well. Use a fork to blend.

> **JUST BEFORE SERVING**

Spread the cheese mixture over the pastry squares. Sprinkle over mint shreds and top each with half a cherry tomato. Reheat for 10 minutes just before serving.

# Roquefort and Cheddar cheese

> makes 20
> preparation time: 20 minutes
> cooking time: 20 minutes

500g (1 lb) ready-made puff pastry dough
1/2 cup crumbled Roquefort cheese
2 tablespoons sour cream or plain yogurt
1 egg yolk
1 cup grated Cheddar cheese

### ❯ CUTTING OUT AND ASSEMBLING

Preheat the oven to 440°F for 20 minutes. Roll out the dough and cut in two equal rectangle shapes.

In a shallow dish, combine the Roquefort and sour cream, or yogurt, and mix well with a fork. Spread this mixture over one pastry rectangle. Top with the other piece of pastry and push down so the pastry sticks together.

### ❯ BEFORE BAKING

Whisk the egg yolk with a little water and brush over the surface of the pastry. Sprinkle with the grated Cheddar, then slice into thin strips. Bake for 15–20 minutes

Note
If you prefer, you can use Emmental or Gruyère.

# Cured beef and cheese pinwheels

> makes 20
> preparation time: 20 minutes
> cooking time: 20 minutes

8 oz ready-made puff pastry dough
3–4 slices thin sliced cured beef, such as bresaola
3–4 slices raclette cheese
1 egg yolk

### ❯ CUTTING OUT AND ASSEMBLING

Preheat the oven to 440°F.

Roll out the pastry dough and trim to a rectangle shape. Top with slices of cured beef, then with slices of cheese. Roll up like a jelly-roll.

### ❯ THE FINISHING TOUCH

Whisk the egg yolk with a little water and brush over the surface of the pastry. Cut the pastry roll into about 20 slices. Line a cookie sheet with baking parchment. Arrange the slices on the sheet and bake for 15–20 minutes.

Note
If raclette cheese is not available, try using Emmental or Gruyère.

# Anchovy cream

makes 20
preparation time: 20 minutes
cooking time: 20 minutes

2 rolls ready-made puff pastry dough
1 tube anchovy paste
1 egg yolk

> **PREPARATION**

Preheat the oven to 440°F for 20 minutes. Roll out the pastry dough and cut out 40 circles with a cookie cutter or small glass.

> **JUST BEFORE SERVING**

Spread some anchovy paste over 20 of the pastry circles, dampen the edges, then top each with another pastry circle and press firmly to seal. Whisk the egg yolk with a little water and brush over the surface of the pastries. Line a cookie sheet with baking parchment. Arrange the pastries on the sheet and bake for 15–20 minutes. Serve hot.

# With fresh peas

makes 20
preparation time: 10 minutes
cooking time: 15 minutes

1 scant cup fresh shelled peas, or frozen peas
4 eggs
1/2 cup milk
olive oil
salt and pepper

> **IN ADVANCE**

Cook the peas in boiling salted water for
10 minutes, less for frozen. Drain well.

> **MEANWHILE...**

Whisk the eggs and milk with a fork and
season with salt and pepper. Heat a little
oil in a nonstick skillet.

> **COOKING**

Put half the peas in the pan with the oil,
then add half of the beaten eggs, which
should just cover the peas.

When the egg mixture is set firm, remove
from the heat to cool. Cook the second
batch in the same way.

Cut the cooled tortillas into 20 squares and
serve cold.

# With red bell peppers

makes 20
preparation time: 30 minutes
cooking time: 15 minutes

1 red bell pepper
4 eggs
1/2 cup milk
olive oil
salt and pepper

> **PEELING THE RED BELL PEPPER**

Cook the bell pepper under a preheated
broiler until the skin is blackened. Put in
a plastic bag, seal well, and allow to cool.
Peel, remove the seeds and core, and cut
into slices.

> **THE TORTILLA...**

Whisk the eggs and milk with a fork and
season with salt and pepper. Heat a little
oil in a nonstick skillet.

Put half the bell pepper slices in the pan and
pour in half of the egg mixture.

When the egg is set firm, remove from the
heat and set aside. Cook the second batch
the same way.

Cut the cooled tortillas into 20 squares and
serve cold.

# Lamb and ginger

makes 20
marinating time: 1 hour
preparation time: 20 minutes
cooking time: 15 minutes

2 tablespoons chopped fresh cilantro
pinch of saffron threads
3 tablespoons grated fresh ginger
1 teaspoon cayenne pepper
1 strip lemon peel
2/3 cup olive oil
3 garlic cloves, crushed
13 oz boneless lamb, cubed
chopped mint, for garnish
salt

> **LEAVE TO MARINATE...**

In a bowl, combine the cilantro, saffron, ginger,
cayenne, lemon peel, olive oil, and garlic.
Season with a little salt. Add the lamb and
toss well. Leave to marinate in the refrigerator
for at least 1 hour.

> **MEANWHILE...**

Light the barbeque or preheat the broiler.
Remove the meat from the marinade and
thread onto flat skewers.

> **AT THE LAST MINUTE**

Broil the kabobs, turning to brown on all
sides, until cooked through, about 10–15
minutes depending on cooking method. Serve
hot, garnished with chopped mint.

# Coconut-honey pork

makes 20
marinating time: 1 hour
preparation time: 20 minutes
cooking time: 15 minutes

1 cup coconut milk
2/3 cup runny honey
7 tablespoons soy sauce
1 tablespoon grated fresh ginger
1 tablespoon chopped fresh cilantro
13 oz boneless pork, cubed
salt and pepper

> **LEAVE TO MARINATE...**

In a bowl, combine the coconut milk, honey,
soy sauce, ginger, and cilantro. Season well, add
the pork and toss well. Leave to marinate in
the refrigerator for at least 1 hour.

> **MEANWHILE...**

Light the barbeque or preheat the broiler.
Remove the meat from the marinade and
thread onto flat skewers.

> **AT THE LAST MINUTE**

Broil the kabobs, turning to brown on all
sides, until cooked through, about 10–15
minutes depending on cooking method.
Serve hot.

# Spicy shrimp

makes 20
marinating time: 1 hour
preparation time: 25 minutes
cooking time: 6 minutes

20 fresh shrimp, deveined
7 table spoons olive oil
Tabasco
cumin seeds
salt and pepper

### ❭ LEAVE TO MARINATE...

Arrange the shrimp side by side
in a dish. Pour over the olive oil,
a few drops Tabasco, and sprinkle
with cumin seeds. Leave to marinate
for 1 hour.

### ❭ MEANWHILE...

Light the barbeque or preheat the
broiler. Remove the shrimp from
the marinade and thread onto flat
skewers or lemon grass stalks.

### ❭ AT THE LAST MINUTE

Grill the shrimp, turning regularly until
cooked through, about 2–3 minutes
each side depending on cooking
method. Serve hot or cold.

# Scallops and bacon

makes 20
marinating time: 1 hour
preparation time: 25 minutes
cooking time: 10 minutes

3 lemons
1 sprig each: thyme, rosemary, sage
1 bay leaf
1 sprig fresh basil leaves snipped with
scissors
1 cup olive oil
20 scallops
20 thin slices smoked bacon
salt and pepper

### ❭ LEAVE TO MARINATE...

In a bowl, combine the juice of all
three lemons, the herbs, bay leaf,
basil, and olive oil. Season with salt
and pepper. Add the scallops, toss
well and leave to marinate in the
refrigerator for 1 hour.

### ❭ AT THE LAST MINUTE

Drain the scallops, then wrap each
in a slice of bacon and secure with
a toothpick. Cook for 10 minutes as
desired depending on method of
cooking (barbeque, ridged grill pan,
broiler or nonstick skillet).

# Chicken satay

makes 20
marinating time: 1 hour
preparation time: 20 minutes
cooking time: 25 minutes

13 oz skinless, boneless,
chicken breast
4 tablespoons soy sauce
4 tablespoons lime juice
1 cup crushed peanuts

**Satay sauce**
1 1/2 cups salted peanuts
3 tablespoons sunflower oil
1 teaspoon grated fresh root ginger
1 3/4 cups coconut milk
3 teaspoons lemon juice
3 teaspoons soy sauce
1 tablespoon Demerara sugar
1/2 teaspoon cayenne pepper

> AT LEAST AN HOUR IN ADVANCE

Slice the chicken thinly and arrange
in a dish. Add the soy sauce and lime
juice and mix well. Leave to marinate
in the refrigerator for at least 1 hour.

> MEANWHILE... THE SATAY SAUCE

Grind the salted peanuts in a small
food processor. Heat the oil in a
small pan, add the peanuts and ginger,
and cook for 2 minutes, stirring
continuously. Add the coconut milk,
lemon juice, soy sauce, sugar, and
cayenne, stirring well to blend.
Lower the heat and simmer gently
until thick, about 10 minutes.

> AT THE LAST MINUTE

Remove the chicken from the
marinade and thread onto flat
skewers. Roll in the crushed peanuts
to coat. Cook on the barbeque,
under the broiler or in a nonstick
skillet, turning until cooked on all
sides. Serve with the sauce.

# Mango-chile duck

makes 20
marinating time: 1 hour
preparation time: 15 minutes
cooking time: 20 minutes

2 skinless, boneless duck breasts
2/3 cup coconut milk
1 jar mango chutney
1 lime
1 strip orange peel
1 small onion, finely chopped
1 red chile, finely chopped
1 garlic clove, crushed
salt and pepper

❯ AT LEAST AN HOUR IN ADVANCE

Cut the duck breasts into 20 equal pieces.
In a bowl, combine the coconut milk,
2 tablespoons of the chutney, the lime juice,
orange peel, onion, chile, garlic, and salt and
pepper. Add the duck pieces, toss well and
leave to marinate for at least 1 hour.

❯ DON'T FORGET...

To preheat, either the barbeque, broiler or
ridged grill pan as necessary. Remove the
duck from the marinade and thread onto
flat skewers.

❯ AT THE LAST MINUTE

Cook the duck, allowing 5–10 minutes per
side. Serve with the remaining mango chutney

# Variations

## Fresh fruit

Add fresh fruit to the kabobs. Mango is the
obvious choice, but peach, nectarine, apple,
or apricot will also work well. Marinate the
fruit of your choice at the same time as
the duck and thread onto skewers, alternating
duck and fruit pieces. Cooking is the same.

## Mango cream dipping sauce

Peel and slice 1 small, ripe mango, then purée
in a food processor. Stir in 3/4 cup light
cream and season with salt and pepper.
Refrigerate until required and serve chilled
with the kabobs.

# Falafel

makes 20
soaking time: 24 hours
preparation time: 15 minutes
cooking time: 15 minutes

7 oz canned chickpeas
7 oz canned fava beans
2 teaspoons baking soda (bicarbonate of soda)
1/2 bunch of parsley, chopped
1/2 bunch of cilantro, chopped
3 tablespoons chopped mint
1 onion
1 garlic clove, crushed
1/2 red chile, minced
1 teaspoon active dry yeast
oil for frying
2 teaspoons salt

### > THE NIGHT BEFORE

Put the chickpeas and fava beans in two separate bowls. Add water to cover and sprinkle each with a spoonful of baking soda.

### > THE NEXT DAY

Drain the chickpeas and fava beans (remove outer skins if you prefer). Put into the bowl of a food processor along with the remaining ingredients and process until smooth.

### > PUT ON YOUR APRON

Form the mixture into small balls. Heat the oil in a pan over medium to high heat. Test with a small amount of the mixture – if it sizzles on top of the oil it is the correct temperature but if it sinks to the bottom of the pan, it is not hot enough. Add the falafel balls and fry, in batches for about 2–3 minutes. Drain on paper towels. Serve hot.

If you need to reheat, pop the balls into a preheated oven at 325°F, or into the microwave.

# Variations

## Shrimp balls

### > IN ADVANCE

In a pan, melt 2 1/2 tablespoons unsalted butter. Gradually stir in 1 cup all-purpose flour. Stir with a wooden spoon until blended. Slowly pour in 2 1/2 cups milk, stirring constantly until the sauce thickens.

In a bowl, combine 2/3 cup chopped peeled shrimp, 1 egg yolk, and 5 1/4 cups grated Cheddar cheese. Season with salt and pepper, stir in the white sauce, and allow to cool.

### > JUST BEFORE SERVING

Form the mixture into 20 small balls. Heat the oil as main recipe. Dip the balls into beaten egg, then into breadcrumbs. Fry until cooked, about 3 minutes. Drain on paper towels and serve hot. Reheat in the oven or microwave if necessary.

## Chicken balls

### > IN ADVANCE

In a food processor, combine: 2 tablespoons sunflower oil, 1 small shallot, 2 garlic cloves, 1 small chile, 1 inch piece of peeled root ginger, grated, 2 teaspoons chopped cilantro, 1 teaspoon fish sauce (nuoc mam). Add 1 cup desiccated coconut and 1 lb skinless, boneless, chicken breast, chopped. Process again until smooth.

### > JUST BEFORE SERVING

Form the mixture into small balls. Cook under a preheated broiler (or in a nonstick skillet) until cooked on all sides, 15–20 minutes. Serve hot.

*Great* ✗ ✗✗✗

# Twisty pastry sticks

{ makes 20
preparation time: 15 minutes
cooking time: 10 minutes

2 rolls ready-made puff pastry dough
1 egg yolk
1 tablespoon sesame seeds
1 tablespoon poppy seeds
1/2 cup grated Cheddar cheese
1 tablespoon dried oregano
1 tablespoon dried thyme
salt and pepper

> **READY IN NO TIME**

Preheat the oven to 375°F.

Unroll the pastry dough. In a bowl, beat the egg yolk with a little water. Brush the surface of the pastry completely with the beaten egg yolk. Sprinkle with the topping of your choice – sesame seeds, poppy seeds, cheese, oregano, or thyme.

> **GIVE IT A TWIST**

Lightly set the topping by rolling the surface of the pastry gently with a rolling pin. Cut the pastry into strips, 3/4 inch thick. Twist the strips. Line a cookie sheet with baking parchment. Arrange the twists on the sheet and bake until golden, about 10 minutes. Serve warm or cold.

*I used*
*Cheddar & Ham 8/06*

# Variations

## With ham

Finely chop some ham. Roll out the pastry and brush with beaten egg yolk as before. Sprinkle with the ham and season with salt and pepper. Add dried herbs if desired (thyme, basil, oregano) and roll gently with a rolling pin to set the topping. Cut into strips, twist, and bake.

## With nuts

In a food processor, coarsely grind some nuts: almonds, hazelnuts, or peanuts. Roll out the pastry and brush with beaten egg yolk as before. Sprinkle with the nuts and season with salt and pepper. Roll with a rolling pin to set the topping. Cut into strips, twist, and bake.

## With Szechuan peppercorns

Coarsely grind a handful of Szechuan peppercorns. Sprinkle over the pastry, which has been brushed with a mixture of beaten egg yolk and water. Season with salt. Roll with a rolling pin to set the topping. Cut into strips, twist, and bake.

# Paprika almonds

serves 8
preparation time: 5 minutes
cooking time: 5 minutes

2 cups whole blanched almonds
paprika
salt

〉 SO SIMPLE

Dry-fry the almonds and paprika in a nonstick skillet, stirring with a wooden spoon. Stop cooking as soon as the nuts turn golden.
Transfer the nuts to a shallow dish and season with salt.

# Five-spice peanuts

serves 8
preparation time: 5 minutes
cooking time: 5 minutes

2 cups whole skinned peanuts
five-spicepowder
salt

〉 TOAST IN THE PAN

Dry-fry the peanuts and five-spice powder in a nonstick skillet, stirring with a wooden spoon. Stop cooking as soon as the nuts turn golden.
Transfer the nuts to a shallow dish and season with salt. Serve in small paper cones.

# Cinnamon hazelnuts

serves 8
preparation time: 5 minutes
cooking time: 5 minutes

2 cups whole skinned hazelnuts
cinnamon
salt

〉 SURE TO PLEASE

Dry-fry the hazelnuts and cinnamon in a nonstick skillet, stirring with a wooden spoon. Stop cooking as soon as the nuts turn golden.
Transfer the nuts to a shallow dish and season with salt. Serve in small paper cones.

# Variations

Any kind of nuts can be used with this preparation. Try macadamias, pecans, etc., and experiment with different flavorings such as curry, cardamom, sesame seeds or ginger.

**Bresaola:** cured dried beef from Italy, available in the delicatessen sections of most large supermarkets. The Swiss version is known as viande des Grisons.

**Chorizo:** a Spanish sausage, usually made from pork or beef. It is highly seasoned and quite spicy and can be eaten as the main ingredient, or added to cooked dishes, such as omelets or paella.

**Chutney:** one of the pioneers of fusion food, this ingredient is an Anglo-Indian staple. It is usually made from vegetables or fruit cooked in vinegar with sugar and spices. The texture is very similar to that of fruit preserves.

**Cilantro:** a highly aromatic herb valued for its seeds as much as its leaves. It is widely used in North African, Asian, Caribbean and Latin American cooking. The herb is sometimes also known as Chinese parsley. The seeds are known as coriander.

**Coconut milk:** an essential ingredient for many curries, this can be obtained in cans from most supermarkets.

**Dill:** popular in both North Africa and Scandinavia, this herb has a flavor whichthat is similar to anise. Use the leaves fresh, not dried, to enhance fish dishes, especially salmon.

**Feta:** a Greek specialty, this cheese is made from sheep or goats' milk. It is ideal in salads, but also in cooked dishes, especially those made with eggplant.

**Five-spice powder:** a Chinese condiment made from a combination of star anise, fennel, clove, cinnamon and Szechuan pepper.

**Ginger:** it is the root that is eaten, not the plant, and it is valued for its peppery, lemony taste. It should be bought fresh and peeled and grated before use.

**Gorgonzola:** one of the most well known of the Italian blue cheeses. It is very rich and slightly piquant.

**Mirin:** a sweet rice wine, from Japan, used in the preparation of sushi. It can be found in many large supermarkets as well as specialty stores.

**Ossau-Iraty:** a well-known sheep's milk cheese that comes from the Pyrénées region of France. Its production is classified (AOC) to ensure high quality.

**Parmesan:** a hard, crumbly Italian grating cheese, the best kind is called Parmesan Reggiano, and has a pleasant, fruity taste. It can be finely grated or shaved into 'curls'.

**Phyllo pastry:** a thin, flaky pastry used in many Mediterranean cuisines, usually filled and deep-fried. Available from most supermarkets and delicatessens.

**Pink peppercorns:** the small dried berries of a rose tree native to South America and not a true pepper. Their use is more visual than culinary, but they add pleasant crunch and a slight peppery taste.

**Poppy seeds:** a common ingredient in the cooking of Central Europe, these seeds are also used to decorate pastries or sprinkled on top of bread rolls and small savory buns. They can be found in large supermarkets or in health food stores.

**Raclette Cheese:** a nutty-flavored cheese made in Switzerland from cows'-milk. It is similar to Gruyère in flavor and also has the distinctive small holes. Specialty cheese stores and good supermarkets will stock it.

**Sesame seeds:** these can be eaten as they come, or lightly toasted, and are also used to make sesame oil. They are used worldwide in cooking, for decoration as well as for flavoring. They can be found in large supermarkets or in health food stores.

**Soy sauce:** the ubiquitous oriental seasoning, found in all supermarkets in a variety of flavor strengths.

**Stilton:** another example of a blue-veined cheese, made from cows' milk. The texture is creamy, with a strong flavor.

**Szechuan peppercorns:** not really a 'pepper' as such (the berries come from a Chinese prickly ash tree), though they do come from the Chinese province of Szechuan. The berries are dried and have a spicy, floral taste.

**Tapenade:** a specialty from Provence, France, this is a ground olive paste, usually made from black olives, sometimes mixed with anchovies. It is available in many large supermarkets and specialty food stores.

**Wasabi:** a very spicy Japanese condiment, available in paste or powder form, made from a root, much like horseradish. Has the same shock tactics.

Shopping: Emery & Cie

© Marabout 2001
text © Thierry Rouissillon
photographs © Akiko Ida

© Hachette 2001
This edition © 2003 Hachette Illustrated UK,
Octopus Publishing Group,
2–4 Heron Quays, London E14 4JP
English translation by JMS Books LLP
(email: moseleystrachan@blueyonder.co.uk)
Translation © Octopus Publishing Group

A CIP catalogue for this book is available from the British Library

ISBN: 1 84430 044 7

Printed by Toppan Printing Co., (HK) Ltd.